Cycling...

Patrick Fillion

L'Aventurine

Translation: William Wheeler
Photographs: Robert Canault

© L'Aventurine, Paris, 2000
ISBN 2-914199-08-2

Contents

Prologue   5
Before 1900 or the Prehistory of cycling   6
Women's bicycles on the road to emancipation   12
Children's bikes   14
Tricycles   15
Tandems   16
Prone-position bicycles   18
Curiosities   19
Track and racing cycles   20
Jack of all trades   22
Hirondelle bicycles   26
Bicycle manufacturers   28
Cycle plaques   32
Manufacturers' catalogues   34
Tire advertisements   38
Tools and equipment   40
Jerseys   44
Eat, drink and pedal   46
Track racing   48
Musical cycles   52
Cycles and the press   58
The legendary Fausto Coppi   63
Pictures big and small   66
The selling of a champion   68
For the younger fans   70
Games and toys   73
Figurines   79
Blotters   84
Cycling and decorative plates   88
Up in smoke   90
A last one for the road   92
Bibliography, useful addresses   93

Prologue

2 a.m. Time to get up.

Every July, the same ritual is performed by hundreds of thousands of people throughout France. Head to the mountains, either the Alps or the Pyrenees. Find a strategically located spot. Wait for hours in the hot sun or pouring rain. Upon seeing the first official on a motorcycle, go into an adrenalin-charged trance.

This magic state is short-lived. Appeased and elated, the disciples return to their cars. Every July, hundreds of thousands of fans watch the *Tour de France* pedal by during one of the mountain stages.

Cycling arouses passionate emotions with only fleeting moments of fulfillment in return. Except for cyclists. Collections are born of these frustrations. The first item is a racing cap or a water bottle discarded on the side of the road. Without realizing it, the simple act of picking up a souvenir started rolling the wheels of the infernal collecting machine. He will soon want other cult objects, other caps, then all the caps of all the teams.

Dealers know how to feed this growing need. The merchants of the Temple of Bicycles have created numerous series of collectibles for them: posters, stickers, games, figurines, records, cigars, matchboxes, glasses, mugs, plates…

The cyclist has not been forgotten. He can buy his favorite champion's bicycle and jersey, and his idol's helmet and shoes.

With his ever-widening experience, the collector becomes more demanding. What he has already accumulated seems suddenly too pedestrian, too easily acquired. He now has his heart set on finding a 19th century velocipede or the 1898 edition of the Manufacture Française d'Armes et Cycles de Saint-Étienne catalogue (the Saint-Étienne Gun and Bicycle Factory).

2 a.m. Time to get up.

Set out for the other side of the country in hopes of acquiring a precious object, the missing one, which a well-paid informer has pointed out in an auction catalogue. Then return home broken-hearted. For want of a few dollars, a richer, more audacious collector carried off the coveted item. Sink into a deep depression. Find new hope when another well-paid informer points out the same item in another sale… Set out again in search of it.

Money isn't an issue – but money is always an issue. It's essential. The collector must sacrifice some of his pieces in order to purchase a more precious one. He must also sacrifice his spare-time activities to save money. He must either sacrifice his family or allow them to share his obsession. The passion has become pathological and the situation borders on the tragic.

The collector now a specialist in his field, becomes a certified expert. The next step is selling. Easy enough. Ten phone calls are all it takes. To the ten people in the country or around the world who may be interested in the object. They all know each other. They have all painfully parted with items they truly love to be able to keep collecting and also to make room.

Lack of space is a serious problem. An entire room is set aside for the incredible *bric-à-brac*, but it is never really large enough for the constantly growing collection. In the best of cases, the collector convinces the city council to loan him premises to open a museum as a fitting tribute to this lifetime collection.

Visitors are touched by a well-worn tricycle. A child visiting the museum thinks of the child who happily rode it in years past. Parents are amused by the rudimentary draisene and impressed by the ingenuity of the velocipedes. In another showcase, they try to recognize which racing caps belong to which cyclists. And then they remember the caps they found on the side of the road at the last *Tour de France*. Why not start a collection?

2 a.m. Time to get up.

Before 1900 or the Prehistory of cycling

The French can be justifiably proud. The "two wheeler" was invented by a Frenchman. In 1791, Count de Sivrac constructed a machine called the celeripede composed of a beam with a wheel connected to each end. The user moved forward by pushing it with his feet, hence the name of the machine.

Or that is how the story, most probably a late 19th century myth, goes. At the same period, Germany had just conquered France and annexed Alsace and Lorraine. If they were also to claim the invention of the bicycle, it would be more than the French could bear. Nonetheless, Baron Karl Friedrich Drais de Sauerbrun did add a decisive improvement to Count de Sivrac's real or imaginary machine. The drive became directional with a pivoting front wheel. The draisene or velocipede, however, was still propelled by the feet.

The third improvement resulting in a machine distantly related to the bicycle can be attributed to Pierre Michaux, a locksmith and carriage manufacturer. In 1861, while he was repairing a draisene, he added cranks or pedals to the front wheel. This invention would also be contested by another Frenchman, Gailloux. He too would have had the same idea and prior to Michaux. Still another compatriot, Pierre Lallemant, would obtain the first patent for a velocipede with pedals. In any case, Pierre Michaux is the only one to have a statue erected to his memory, in his hometown of Bar-le-Duc. Since the Germans had just erected a monument commemorating Baron Drais' invention, for the French, it was a question of national pride and keeping up with neighbors.

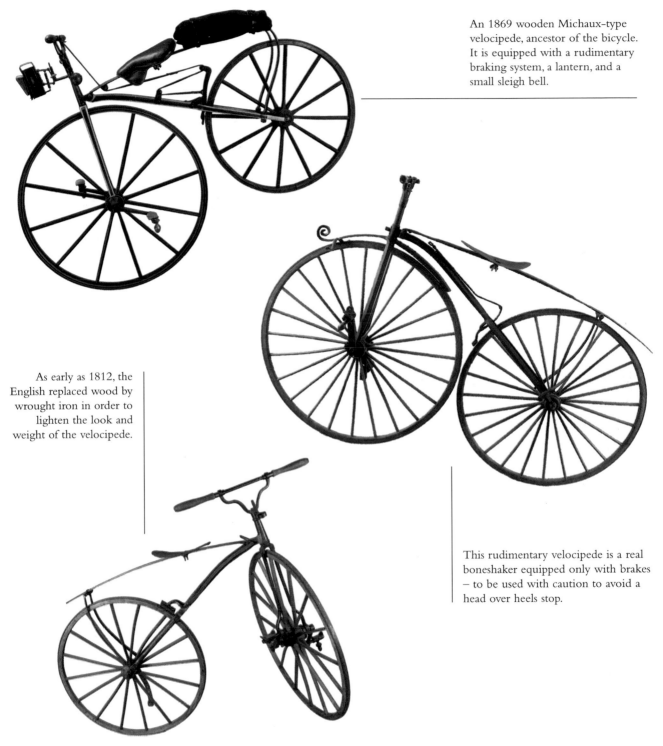

An 1869 wooden Michaux-type velocipede, ancestor of the bicycle. It is equipped with a rudimentary braking system, a lantern, and a small sleigh bell.

As early as 1812, the English replaced wood by wrought iron in order to lighten the look and weight of the velocipede.

This rudimentary velocipede is a real boneshaker equipped only with brakes — to be used with caution to avoid a head over heels stop.

In 1872, an Englishman, James Starley, invented the penny-farthing. The diameter of the front wheel sometimes attained 1.5 meters in diameter. Each turn of the pedal advanced the machine proportionately and the small back wheel served mostly as counterbalance. This model was created in 1880 by Adolphe Clement, an apprentice locksmith who produced high quality machines. Note the rung above the back wheel to help the rider reach the seat.

Velocipedes caused many accidents. Founded in February, 1881, the French Velocipedic Association issued a velocipede license obtained after training on a special indoor track and passing a road test.

In an attempt to improve its stability, the seat of the penny-farthing was lowered. The use of metal spokes and general developments in metallurgical techniques, resulted in the production of racing models weighing less than ten kilos.

More effective but too high

The rider on a penny-farthing, with its pedals almost vertically aligned with the seat, could adopt a more efficient position than on the velocipede which required stretching his legs forward. Nonetheless, these tall machines were perilous to operate; with each turn of the pedal, they pitched to the left or right. Sitting high permitted the rider to dominate the pedestrians around him and to avoid puddles and mud holes unless he fell… As the machine picked up speed, he had to remove his feet from the pedals which certainly did not increase stability. To remedy these problems, John Starley decided to lower the center of gravity and to do this, both wheels had to be of almost identical size. Presented in 1885, his Rover Safety resembled a modern bicycle.

Many potential cyclists shied away from velocipedes and penny-farthings because they were considered dangerous. In 1863, Pierre and Ernest Michaux created a more stable three-wheeler. It appealed to less experienced riders and especially to women who had fewer problems with large skirts when sitting on a lowered seat.

This surprisingly modern-looking bicycle dates from 1891. It has a t-bar frame: the bar linking the steering to the hub of the back wheel crosses another linking the seat to the crank gear. It is also equipped with the latest improvements: tangent spokes (invented by John Starley in 1874), roller chain (invented by Hans Renold in 1879), ball bearings (invented by Jules Pierre Surivay in 1869). But what really makes it modern is its rear-wheel drive.

Some manufacturers attempted to eliminate the chain. On this 1897 Chereau-type bicycle, an intermediate gear transmits the force from the pedal sprocket to the back wheel hub.

11

Stella women's model in Duraluminium. This alloy was used in the years prior to World War II. Bicycles principally made of it were lighter. In 1942, however, the occupied French were forbidden to use such alloys and steel had to be used for manufacturing bicycles and inferior quality steel at that. Fortunately for manufacturers, demand was high. Stella bicycles became famous when Louison Bobet won the *Tour de France* on one of its models.

Cover of a Manufacture Française d'Armes et Cycles de Saint-Étienne catalogue. The message here is that a girl on a bike can easily escape the grips of even the most athletic boy on foot.

Women's bicycles on the road to emancipation

The development of bicycles contributed to women's autonomy. For the first time they had an individual means of transportation progressively accessible to all social classes as prices decreased. Riding a bicycle wearing a long dress or skirt was not very easy; the cross bar had already been eliminated on women's models to help the situation. Moreover, cycling inspired clothes which would also contribute to the social evolution of women. At the end of the 19th century, a type of pants suit with a long jacket was available for women cyclists. Many men (and women) however considered this indecent apparel. Forty years later, when automobiles had already started to supplant bicycles, German occupation of France and wartime gas rationing obliged women to return to mechanical means of transportation. Even the most wealthy women did not hesitate to use bicycles, obliging fashion designers to keep up with the times. Culottes became all the rage especially when worn with a three-quarter length, multi-pocketed and often hooded jacket, so practical for those long daily shopping trips.

A teenage girl always has things to carry around. That is why this bike is outfitted with a wicker basket carryall behind the seat.

A Cressent bike produced by one of the innumerable French manufacturers.

Children's models allowed very young girls to learn to ride. If in the beginning, cycling was only practised by a few pioneer women, later generations of females were confirmed cyclists from a very early age on.

On this 1925 model, the metallic webbing around the upper part of the back wheel prevents skirts from being caught in the spokes.

Childrens' bikes

The young owner of this tricycle can be justifiably proud. It resembled those ridden by adults, including his mother's. They can now cycle together in the park.

To familiarize the young child (during the second half of the 19th century) with the workings of cycles, he was seated on this hobby horse with pedals. This model also brings to mind the hopes of velocipede inventors who wanted to create the "poor man's horse".

Finally a bike like Dad's. This 1891 children's model is an exact replica of the adult version. It is however not exactly the "poor man's horse". At the time it cost 180 francs whereas the yearly salary of a postman (who delivered mail on a bicycle) was 500 francs.

Tricycles

Monet-Guyon is a legendary name known to all motorcycle enthusiasts. This make existed from 1917 to 1958 and a number of models are still in running condition. They also produced automobiles.

At the end of World War I, Joseph Monet and Adrien Guyon wanted to help disabled veterans to be independant and rediscover a taste for life. The two manufacturers had them in mind when they invented the "vélocimane". This rare 1926 model was easily converted: the crank gear, footrests, handcranks and handlebars were interchangeable.

This type of bicycle was used on Ré Island, off the French Atlantic coast, until the 1950's. Women in particular used it to go to work in the salt marshes.

This practical 1935 Auguste Treff model has two front wheels and was designed for riders with poor balance. It has back-pedal breaks.

Tandems

This side-by-side tandem of course had two inventors, Noël and Captain Gérard. It was used by army and police patrols as well as by couples.

In 1936, thanks to the Popular Front government headed by Leon Blum, the French had their first paid vacation. Thousands bought tandem bikes (the one presented is a L. Lesschaeve model). Workers and employees had two weeks to discover their country; thanks to bicycles and camping, they enjoyed the new sensations of leisure time and traveling for pleasure.

That same year with tandems all the rage, Delangle Bicycle Co. publicized the recent hour record set by Richard and Dayen on one of their models: 48.668 kilometers. On the flyer, Maurice Richard (with more than thirty personal records from the 2 mile to the 70 kilometer) added in his own hand a reminder of his proudest moment: his individual hour record of 45.298 kilometers set at the Vigorelli cycle track in Milano, Italy on October 14. In 1955, the track was remeasured and Richard's distance was diminished to 45.325 kilometers. The moral of the story is that two on a bicycle go faster than one but only 3.343 kilometers faster per hour.

Prone-position bicycles

Victor Sironval built this cycle with a metal knuckle steering system in 1939. Only two thousand models were manufactured. The cyclist pedaled in a semi-recumbent position.

Lying down at the wheel

The idea dated from 1933. Charles Mochet invented a bicycle where the cyclist pedaled in a prone position. It seemed at first to be just another whacky idea from bikeland. A friend of the inventor, Francis Faure, decided to show everyone just how sensible it actually was by attempting to beat Oscar Egg's seemingly unattainable hour distance record set in 1914. The old hour record fell with a surprising 45.055 kilometer performance by Faure. This turn of events left the sporting powers quite perplexed. One of the roles of the International Cycling Federation was to validate new records. After a close vote, it was decided to refuse Faure's record. Moreover, prone position bicycles were barred from normal competition. Still today, misfits continue to build "horizontal" bicycles and their hour distance record has almost attained 80 kilometers. Chris Boardman holds the current record on a regular cycle with 56.375 kilometers, covered in an hour.

Curiosities

Early 19th century circus cycle, probably a converted draisene.

Recent penny-farthing dating from the Seventies. This front-wheel drive machine has an interesting transmission system. The chain turns two sprockets in the center of the large front wheel.

Track and racing cycles

Well before the end of the 19th century, turned-down handlebars were standard equipment on racing bicycles. A cyclist pedaling sitting straight up on the seat offers more resistance to the wind which slows him down. However, if he leans forward, his crouched position improves aerodynamics and his speed increases for the same effort.

Bernard Hinault is one of the greatest living cycling champions. During his career, he trained in a windtunnel offseason in order to find the best aerodynamic position possible. This experience was invaluable not only to him personally but to perfect the cycles that were commercialized under his name.

JAN DERKSEN
Wereldkampioen Sprint
Professionals 1957
Berijder der alom bekende Radium tubes

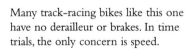

Many track-racing bikes like this one have no derailleur or brakes. In time trials, the only concern is speed.

Jack of all trades

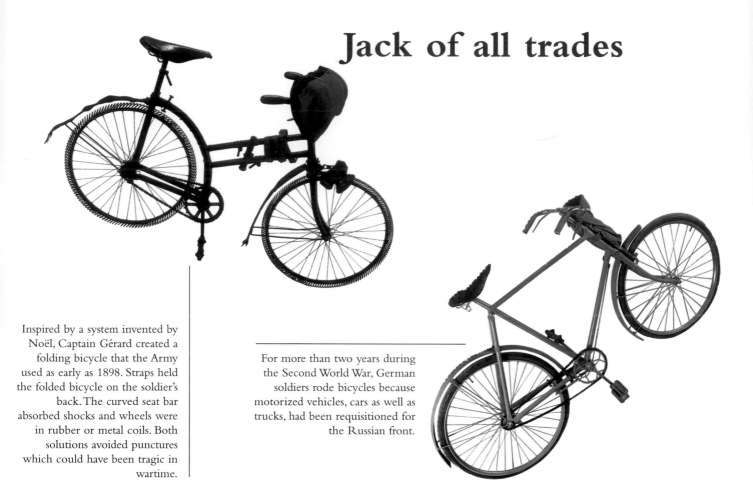

Inspired by a system invented by Noël, Captain Gérard created a folding bicycle that the Army used as early as 1898. Straps held the folded bicycle on the soldier's back. The curved seat bar absorbed shocks and wheels were in rubber or metal coils. Both solutions avoided punctures which could have been tragic in wartime.

For more than two years during the Second World War, German soldiers rode bicycles because motorized vehicles, cars as well as trucks, had been requisitioned for the Russian front.

As early as 1830, a visionary postal worker realized what an incredible tool draisenes could be for rural mail delivery. The administration used them for a trial period but cut short the test because of problems encountered in bad weather. This was in the pre-Michaux days when such machines had neither cranks nor pedals. It wasn't until the 1880's that their use by the postal service became effective, with the first bicycles equipped with inflatable tires developed by Dunlop. Several years later, Captain Gérard would champion the cause of the bicycle to military officials. He favored the creation of infantry corps equipped with bicycles. His idea was finally adopted and these corps would play an important role during the First World War in delivering dispatches and in enemy troop surveillance.

The utilitarian uses of cycles multiplied notably with the introduction of the Hirondelle models produced by the Manufacture Française d'Armes et Cycles de Saint-Étienne.

Professions of all kinds making deliveries found the appropriate model in this renowned company's specialized catalogue. The carrier tricycles, for example, were capable of transporting weights exceeding several hundred kilos.

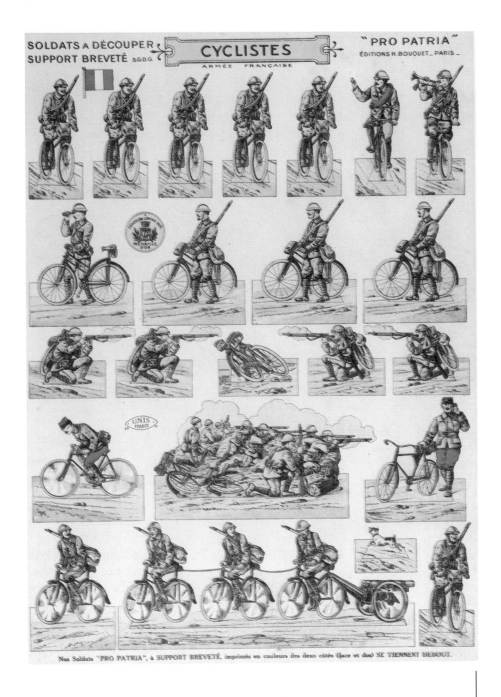

To encourage patriotic fervor in children, cardboard sheets of cutout figures, "printed in color on both sides and with flaps to stand figures upright", presented the various ways bicycles were used by the Army. Folded on his back, the bicycle did not hinder a soldier from firing his rifle. Perched on it, he could observe enemy troops or lead the charge with a bugle call. Three bicycles combined could pull a cannon. But one question was cause for a debate: should the "mounted" infantry be allowed to wear the red trousers reserved for the line infantry?

Parachutists were occasionally equipped with folding bicycles allowing them to leave their landing point quickly.

During the war cyclists had to modify lighting for night riding. The glass cover was blackened except for a thin band in the middle in order to prevent enemy planes from locating bicycles. The licence plate on the back fender was obligatory during the Occupation.

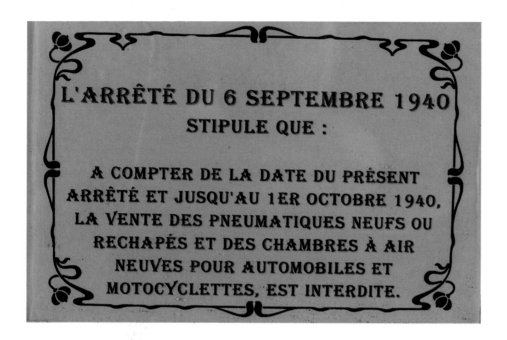

L'ARRÊTÉ DU 6 SEPTEMBRE 1940
STIPULE QUE :

A COMPTER DE LA DATE DU PRÉSENT
ARRÊTÉ ET JUSQU'AU 1ER OCTOBRE 1940,
LA VENTE DES PNEUMATIQUES NEUFS OU
RECHAPÉS ET DES CHAMBRES À AIR
NEUVES POUR AUTOMOBILES ET
MOTOCYCLETTES, EST INTERDITE.

During several weeks in September, 1940, the sale of new and retreaded tires was suspended. Resourceful cyclists soon found a solution. Discs of cork and rubber were strung on a metal wire around the wheel rim. This allowed those who depended on bicycle for transportation to keep rolling.

This 1935 model had a
backpedaling feature
which facilitated ascents.

Hirondelle bicycles

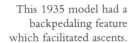

For her, a wide-tire
Hirondelle for a
comfortable ride even
on rut-filled country
roads, the perfect place
for picking wildflowers.
For him, a Hirondelle
with racing handlebars.

Dependable bicycles

Hirondelle bicycles were produced in Saint-Étienne since 1893. The make was
later continued by the Manufacture Française d'Armes et Cycles in the same
city. It remained one of the most popular and best-loved makes throughout the
first half of the 20th century until production ceased after the Second World
War. Police departments all over France were equipped with this make and
became so identified with it that the nickname for policemen was "hirondelle"
(swallow in French).

RÉTRO-DIRECTE HIRONDELLE A 4 VITESSES

GRAND PRIX du T. C. F.

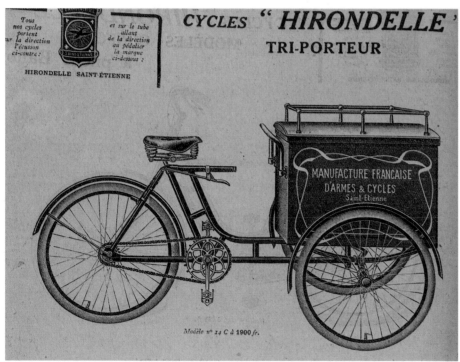

This page from the Manufacture Française d'Armes et Cycles de Saint-Étienne catalogue shows a 4-speed Hirondelle, the traditional gift for students having passed their first important certificate for elementary studies.

This three-wheel chest carrier was a popular delivery model with food and beverage merchants.

Bicycle manufacturers

CYCLES Peugeot 1931

This bicycle was built near the city of Valentigny in the Franche-Comté in 1903, the year of the first *Tour de France*. The 2,428 kilometer long race was won by Maurice Garin with an average speed of 25.679 kilometers per hour. Two years later, Louis Trousselier won both the *Tour* and the grueling Paris-Roubaix race on a Peugeot.

In the late 19th century, Peugeot, Japy and Company produced saws and other carpentry tools, skirt hoops and umbrella ribs. In 1882, the first industrially manufactured bicycle, a penny-farthing, rolled off its assembly lines. In 1892, Peugeot launched the "Lion" make for bicycles. This animal is still used today for the logo.

Even in the days before marketing, bicycle manufacturers were well aware of the importance of a good name and its metaphorical impact to vaunt the incredible capabilities of their machines. The griffon is a mythical animal with the body of a lion and the head and wings of an eagle. The greyhound is known for its speed in catching small game and on race tracks.

Although the Manufacture Française d'Armes et Cycles de Saint-Étienne dominated the bicycle market, many smaller manufacturers were located in the greater Paris region. Many of them chose to set up shop near the first Buffalo cycling track, after Porte Maillot. This was the case for Chabrier cycles located in nearby Clichy.

Cleveland was one of the
foremost American bicycle
manufacturers in the beginning
of the 20th century. Lucien
Lesna's victory in the 1901
Paris–Bordeaux race boosted
their reputation in Europe.

Cycle plaques

Screwed on the head bar, bicycles plaques provided an excellent opportunity for the manufacturer to show his imagination. Mythological characters were one source of inspiration.

Animals of all types were obvious subjects for logos. They possessed the speed and force often identified with bicycles.

Plaques are standard equipment on bicycles all over the world. This one is from the Ivory Coast in Africa where cycles are a popular means of transportation.

Maurice Garin's victory in the first *Tour de France* in 1903 publicized the prestigious La Française Diamant make.

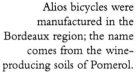

Alios bicycles were manufactured in the Bordeaux region; the name comes from the wine-producing soils of Pomerol.

Well before Terminator, there was Liberator. It was the name of the American bomber widely used during the Second World War and a French bicycle make. The cross of Lorraine figures on the plaque of Lorraine bicycles and brings to mind General De Gaulle and the Liberation of France in 1945.

In the beginning, Valentigney, the town where the first factory was located, was inscribed on Peugeot plaques. When the company offices moved to Paris, the plaque design was modified. The lion was doubly appropriate, figuring both on the coat of arms of the province of Franche-Comté and as the logo for the original Peugeot, Japy Steel Company.

Favor was a make of bicycles established in Clermont-Ferrand which also produced motorized cycles and motorcycles. Its motto was "Favor goes straight to the point."

Manufacters' catalogues

At the turn of the 20th century, a multitude of small bicycle manufacturers sprung up although few would succeed. One way of standing out in the crowd was a distinctive catalogue. The most obvious cover illustrations featured bicycles or, at the very least, a wheel. The message of the J.C Cycle Company catalogue is more explicit: Cyclists are riding on a country road.
One of them (of course on a J.C bicycle) has such a lead that he has stopped to let the others catch up.

Louvet Bicycles chose a she-wolf (*louve* in French) as its logo for the play on words.

The bicycle is an inexpensive way of ensuring freedom of movement. It also replaces the horse. This would seem to be the symbolic message of the Bella Bicycle catalogue where a torch-carrying Liberty is riding a fiery charger.

Nothing looks more like the globe of the world than a bicycle wheel. The cover of the rules book of the French Velocipede Federation used the comparison to underline its role. Like the mythological Atlas, it supports the world of bicycles. A disturbing griffon-like beast is the guardian to the inner sanctum.

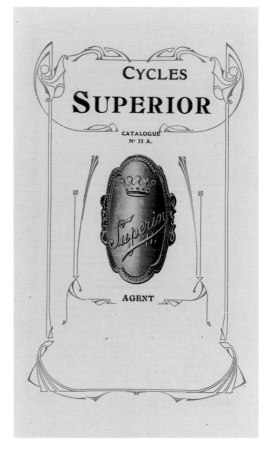

Certain bicycle manufacturers survived because they diversified production to include motorcycles. This was the case for both Favor and Automoto – the latter clearly announcing its dual ambitions in its name. It was equally the case for Superior Bicycles, a British company with agents in France whose motorcycles still attract collectors.

Created in the 1890's in the region of Lyon, the Rochet Bicycle Company
was established by a family of stonecutters. They considered bicycles to be part of the future and participated directly in their development with the first wheels with wire spokes.

Wolber Bicycles have not been produced for many years although Michelin continued to use the brand name for tires, especially retreads, until 1999.

The catalogue of all catalogues was, of course, the Manufacture Française d'Armes et Cycles de Saint-Étienne catalogue. The company at times totalized more than 75 per cent of bicycle sales in France. Their general catalogue continued to grow until it reached 1,100 pages, 30,000 illustrations and more than 1.5 kilos in weight. It was later divided into several separate catalogues.

Tire advertisements

The Michelin brothers invented the inner tube in 1891. Édouard created a dismountable tire attached to the rim by simple bolts. These and other inventions helped the company prosper. In 1897, Bibendum, their publicity symbol, was born through a series of coincidences. This fat figure was such a godsend that he is still universally recognizable today. During an 1893 conference, André Michelin came up with a catchy phrase: "Tires drink obstacles." One day the two brothers were looking at a pile of tires of different dimensions and noticed how human they appeared, only the arms were missing. An illustrator showed them a series of projects he had designed for other customers. One showed a very rotond German raising his beer stein and shouting *"Nunc est bidendum"* (It's time to drink). It came to André Michelin in a flash, combining his slogan "Tires drink obstacles" and the figure made of tires. Michelin gave precise indications to the illustrator Marius Rossillon. On the first poster, Bibendum is shown downing a cup filled with pieces of glass and nails. His exclamation *"Nunc est bidendum"* is translated by "To your health. Michelin drinks obstacles." Bibendum was born. Since these ads principally targeted automobile owners, Bibendum's accessories – a signet ring, eye glasses and cigar – reflect the social class of those who can afford such a purchase. Not surprisingly, they are also those of André Michelin.

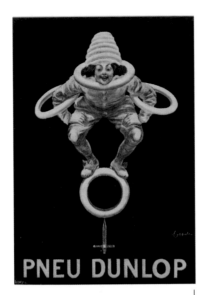

John Boyd Dunlop, a veterinarian of Scottish origin, invented the tire in 1888. The idea for the inflatable tire came to him when he saw what difficulty his son had riding his tricycle. The first version was an air-filled rubber tube inside a rubberized canvas casing nailed onto a large wooden disk. The first tire factory opened in Dublin in 1889. That same year, Gustave Clément, a bicycle and automobile manufacturer, acquired the license for France and opened the first production unit in Levallois, near Paris. In order to keep up with the rapid development of the automobile, Dunlop France opened a second production unit in Montluçon in 1919. Advertising was important for the company since the competition from its main rival Michelin was intense.

The Hutchinson Tire Company also had its Bibendum, although it never enjoyed the same success. He resembled Uncle Sam and occasionally appeared dressed in extravagant polka dotted overalls. In 1853, the Anglo-American Hiram Hutchinson launched the production of rubber wheels in a former royal paper mill near Montargis. The Hutchinson Tire Company was created at his death in 1898.

Tools and equipment

Manufacturers adapted their products to accomodate the cyclist's saddle pouch underneath the seat. Musts for the cyclist include M.A.F.A.C. brake cables, Brampton chains (the most widely sold make in the world), wrenches and patches to repair blowouts.

Cycling is principally an outdoor sport which means the cyclist is often alone in the middle of nowhere and needs to have basic tools in case of a mechanical breakdown. Specialized shoes are necessary for efficient pedaling. Appropriate apparel does not hinder movement and provides protection during bad weather. They must also keep the cyclist reasonably dry even when he is wet with perspiration.

Cycle races were organized as soon as velocipedes were equipped with pedals. The first dates back to 1868 and covered only several miles, between the Saint-Cloud Park and the Paris city limits. The following year, the Paris-Rouen Race was open to competitors. The specific equipment necessary for races quickly attracted the attention of manufacturers.

Souliers Cyclistes

1002. « Comingman », cuir souple et résistant, spécialement étudié pour les jeunes. Article réclame .. n. **39. »**

1024. « Club », en vachette box noir. Parfait soulier d'entraînement .... **55. »**

1004. « Souchard », type routier avec bride de maintien empêchant le soulier de sortir du pied. Parfait pour le tourisme .... n. **65. »**

1014. « Souchard », type spécial course, forme spéciale très dégagée ..... n. **65. »**

1027. « Service course », modèle spécialement étudié pour la course sur route .. **65. »**

1028. « Le Grèvès », box extra-souple, forme nouvelle, très chaussante. Signée par le Ch. de France 1936 n. **89. »**

1029. « La Médaille », en veau box extra-léger, bordure blanche, cambrure demi-souple, talons croissant. Forme nouvelle légère. Pour la piste .... **75. »**

1030. « Speicher », type champion du monde, box extra-souple, façon cousu main. Modèle extra-léger, étudié pour la course. Adopté par tous les champions de la piste et de la route .. n. **89. »**

> Le plus grand choix - La meilleure qualité
> Les plus bas Prix

The Unis–Sport catalogue carried a full line of cycling equipment each year. Some of their models were sponsored by champions. In the 1938 catalogue, for example, Le Grèves, Speicher, Lapébie and Leducq all had shoes named after them. Cycling was taken seriously by Unis-Sport; so much so, that they themselves sponsored a team headed by Gino Bartali.

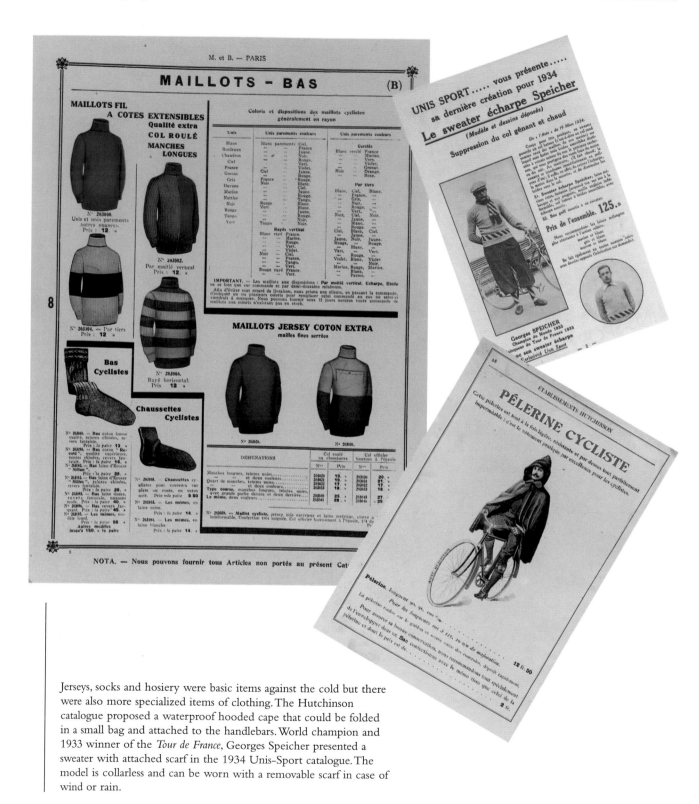

Jerseys, socks and hosiery were basic items against the cold but there were also more specialized items of clothing. The Hutchinson catalogue proposed a waterproof hooded cape that could be folded in a small bag and attached to the handlebars. World champion and 1933 winner of the *Tour de France*, Georges Speicher presented a sweater with attached scarf in the 1934 Unis-Sport catalogue. The model is collarless and can be worn with a removable scarf in case of wind or rain.

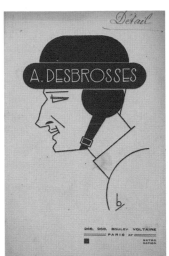

Professional cyclists sometimes throw their caps away during races to the joy of collectors. This is less often the case with helmets although they were very unpopular in France. Racers have gone on strike so that they would not be obliged to wear helmets during competition. In any case, they are the best protection against head injuries. They can also help build a legend. Jean Robic was nicknamed "Leatherhead" because he wore his helmet all the time, on and off his bicycle.

43

Jerseys

For the spectators massed along the road, a cycling race only lasts thirty seconds or less, the time it takes for the pack to pedal by. That is why in 1919 the inventor of the *Tour de France*, Henri Desgrange, came up with the idea of a distinctive bright yellow jersey for the race leader. In that way he would stand out in the blur of colors of the other cyclists. A solid green jersey is worn by the points leader – won in sprints in the different stages – whereas the red polka dot jersey is worn by the best climber. The idea caught on quickly and soon all important stage races followed suit. The red polka dot jersey shown here was won in the 1998 *Tour de France* by Christophe Rinero.

Several jerseys are signed by Hennie Kuiper, one of the best Dutch cyclists. He wore the Ti-Raleigh rainbow jersey during the 1976 season since he was the reigning world champion and the white RMC-Reynolds jersey as leader of the annual Paris-Nice race. Kuiper won the pink jersey sponsored by *La Gazetta dello Sport* in a stage of the *Giro* – the Italian equivalent of the *Tour de France*, although he never won the race. The yellow jersey is proof that he was the race leader of the *Vuelta*, the Spanish equivalent of the *Tour de France*.

The others are team jerseys. Raymond Poulidor and Cyrille Guimard were well-known racers on the Fagor Mercier team. Thanks to Eddy Merckx, the greatest champion in cycling history, the Molteni team will be remembered. The champions Francesco Moser and Giuseppe Saronni both wore the Sanson-Campagnolo jerseys. The last two jerseys illustrate important lessons about sports endorsement. The SEM France-Loire jersey is proof that sponsoring a cycling team is risky; the poor results of the team contributed to the demise of the France-Loire factory. The Chazal-König jersey is covered with the names of the different sponsors. If an additional sponsor was needed to complete the budget, there would be no place for his name!

Eat, drink and pedal

Food satchels are distributed to the racers at fixed spots along the course. Sporting the colors of a sponsor or the race organizers, they are handed out by the support staff of each team. It is quite an impressive sight to see each racer in the pack trying to pick out the satchel-bearing member of their team from the crowd. The racers hardly slow down during the food distribution but empty the contents into the different pouches of their jersey, quickly discarding the cloth satchels along the road side. Nonetheless, the *Tour de France* rule book is emphatic. "In order to prevent a collective fall of the racers, injuries to spectators, or to avoid inciting the latter to cross the road, it is strictly forbidden to discard of food satchels, water bottles or any other accessory imprudently." Whenever a cyclist throws his satchel away, a swarm of spectators descend on it: that is the only way collectors can obtain them.

What's for lunch?

The satchels are handed out two or three hours after the beginning of the race. The food has to be sufficiently calorific to replenish the racers' depleted energy levels in order for them to make it to the end of the race: ham, chicken or turkey sandwiches, rolls, rice cakes, dried fruit, ginger bread, cookies, tartlets, cereal or high energy bars…

Nowadays cyclists can drink as they race thanks to plastic squeeze bottles with easy-opening nozzle tops, light years away from the old metal bottles with cork stoppers. A long time sponsor of the *Tour de France*, the Coca-Cola Company distributes their bottles during races by motorcycle. Of course, they contain… slightly salted water, diluted fruit juice and special high energy liquids and never carbonated beverages.

934. — VÉLODROME BUFFALO. — Une course de grand fond   J. H.

Track racing

Oval cycling race tracks bring to mind chariot races in Roman colosseums. The entertainment world saw the theatrical potential of racing: the director of the Folies Bergère, Clovic Clerc financed the Buffalo, the first race track built on the outskirts of Paris in 1893. It was later demolished and rebuilt in the nearby suburbs. Authors such as the famous playwright Tristan Bernard were fascinated by the high drama of the races – the favorite with a commanding lead falls and suddenly a triumph becomes a tragedy…

France is one of the leading nations of track cyclists. There are currently ninety-eight race tracks in France of which three are indoor. Unfortunately, track races no longer attract the huge crowds they once did. It was the common man's sport although all social classes were present. In Paris, at the Buffalo and the Vélodrome d'Hiver especially during the famous Six Day Race, singers and entertainers liked to perform for the enthusiastic crowds. Large provincial cities all had their race track: memorable marathon races were organized in Marseilles, Nice and Toulouse. Today, nostalgic collectors can reminisce as they look at old postcards and press photos. For cyclists it is an excellent training experience as track racing develops skills which are essential for road races especially learning to survive in a tightly grouped and sprinting pack.

Pierre Mac Orlan and the track

"I was six or seven years old when I visited the Seine cycle track for the first time. I still remember the races with teams of three. The trainers wore the same jerseys as the cyclists, bright colors in an energy-charged atmosphere. Vibrant colors on this circle of passion… Even today, I can still remember the trainers' names of the Gladiator or the Arthur Linton team, the exact place that Robert Coquelle or the then thin Lamberjack occupied. Souvenir, souvenir."

Photos of racetracks are rather standardized, showing the grandstands or the wide curved tracks in Montargis, the Vincennes Park near Paris or in Vichy, near the famous spa.

The Six Days of Paris was the classic indoor
endurance race. One of the cyclists of each of the
two or three member teams had to be on the track
at all times during the 144 hour race. The record was
set by Goulet and Fogler in 1913 who covered
4,467.58 kilometers. The fatigue was so intense, the
competitors literally fell from lack of sleep. Here, the
cyclist Strom has fallen asleep in his cubicle while
waiting for his food. In case of injuries or
exhaustion, doctors and nurses were present at all
times for the competitors and occasionally for
overzealous spectators.

During the Six Days of Paris, a temporary city within the city sprang up beneath the hundreds of lights surrounding the race track built in 1910 near the Seine River. Eating was an important activity for spectators whether they brought picnic lunches or dined in one of the restaurants. There were even accomodations for reporters who spent the six days and nights at the race track. Track officials had the difficult task of counting the number of laps for each team.

Musical cycles

All the well-known champions had records dedicated to their sporting feats. Among them was Louison Bobet who enjoyed immense popularity during his racing career. Raymond Poulidor, the eternal runner-up, had several records dedicated to him even though he never won the *Tour de France*. But for most cyclists, record sales soared only after every important victory. Robert Pingeon, Bernard Thevenet and Bernard Hinault were also honored in music, as well as European champions such as Rik Van Looy, Francesco Moser, Fausto Coppi and Eddy Merckx.

Cycling, popular music and the accordeon go together in France. Well-known singers and musicians enjoyed singing and performing songs to the glory of this working class sport. During the legendary Six Day Race, all eyes were on Le Vel d'Hiv, the famous indoor race track in Paris. Variety acts in the middle of the oval track entertained the spectators (and the racers) with songs especially written for the occasion. That is all a thing of the past although some race tracks like Paris Bercy and Grenoble try to keep the tradition alive. Collectors have only the sheet music as reminders of the great musical past. With the arrival of the 45, the record industry accompanied the ever-flourishing love affair between the *Tour de France* and popular music. Every great champion had his musical tribute engraved in black vinyl. The *Tour* regularly launched new official songs which circulated among the participating members of the caravan. Since the spectators spent long hours waiting, they also picked up the catchy tunes. Cycling being such an immensely popular activity, singers were almost sure of having a hit if they brought out a song related to this sport. This was already true at the beginning of the 20th century.

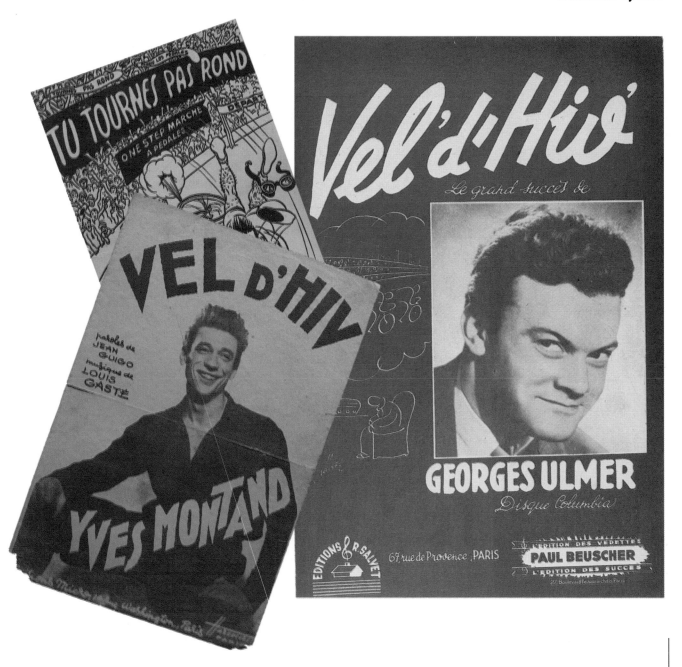

Cycling songs were so popular that sometimes several songs had the same title. *Vel d'Hiv*, in honor of the Paris race track, was sung by Georges Ulmer, (better known for his song *Pigalle*), as well as by the young Yves Montand. The music and lyrics sung by the latter were written by Line Renaud's husband, Loulou Gasté. Orchestras played in shifts to boost the spectators' morale during the endurance races. Music was an integral part of track races.

53

Every year the *Tour de France* put its stamp of approval on one tune which would be considered the offical song for that summer. One of France's best loved accordeon players, Yvette Horner, started her career playing during the different stages of this famous race. She played for long hours standing up in a car with an open roof, an athletic performance in itself.

Cabaret entertainers knew how important cycling was for many Frenchmen. Singing or telling humorous stories about this subject always attracted attention. The famous actor and humorist Bourvil did both. His sketches or *monologues* were brought out on 33's and the texts were published like sheet music complete with stage indications for would-be comedians.

56

The song *Il a crevé son pneu* tells the sad story of love betrayed all because of a flat tire. Eugène and Joséphine were riding their bikes with friends when Eugène had a flat tire. Instead of waiting for him, Joséphine rode off in search of more able company. The second verse even suggests that Eugène's flat might reflect a lack of sexual prowess. Despite his efforts, he couldn't inflate his tire and when he returned home, everyone in the village made fun of him. Moral of the story: carry an extra inner tube and a pump if you want to keep your girlfriend.

Cycles and the press

At the turn of the 20th century, two sports dailies, *Vélo* and *L'Auto* were furious adversaries. To pick up circulation during the summer months, Henri Desgranges, director of *L'Auto*, had the crazy idea with Géo Lefèvre to create a six-stage cycling race throughout France. At first there were few competitors and the rules were rather fuzzy but it was the birth of a legend. *L'Auto* doubled its sales and several months later *Vélo* closed shop.

Long before live television transmission and even before live radio coverage, cycling fans followed racing results in the written press. Since many races had been especially created by newspaper owners to boost sales and since they were authentic sporting feats – the ascent of a mountain pass in the Alps or the Pyrenees on a gravel road –, the tone of articles was extravagant. Superlatives were never lacking. Writing in 1953, Jacques Goddet, director of the *Tour de France* and the sports daily *L'Équipe*, expressed it in the following manner: "Although the grandiloquence of the journalists covering the *Tour* causes literary purists to wince and armchair athletes to smile, they maintain the heroic character of this war on wheels." Journalists such as Gaston Bénac, Albert Baker d'Isy, Pierre Chany and Antoine Blondin largely contributed to the mythification of the great cycling champions. This impassioned relationship between the press and professional cycling was almost born with the sport. Founded by Richard Lesdide in 1869, the newspaper *Le Vélocipède illustré* was one of the organizers of the first true bicycle race in France, the Paris-Rouen. Nowadays, articles are more analytical and the specialized press has almost completely disappeared.

Cycling is good for newspaper sales. *Le Petit journal illustré* organized the Paris-Brest-Paris race. *Le Chasseur français* was owned by the Manufacture Française d'Armes et Cycles de Saint-Étienne. Cover illustrations regularly featured cycling which was good for bicycle sales.

L'Équipe began where *L'Auto* left off. The latter was obliged to cease publication after the Second World War because it had continued normal activities under German occupation. Cycling enthusiasts resumed their love affair with the *Tour de France*'s first post-war race in 1947. The Breton Jean Robic won the last stage and the *Tour*. *L'Équipe* sold more and more newspapers every summer. Louison Bobet's three victories were also great boosts for circulation.

The cycling craze of the Thirties favored the creation of cycling magazines. Great French champions such as André Leducq, Antonin Magne and René Vietto inflamed crowds of spectators. Photos taken during the stages were transmitted to home offices using state of the art technology, telephotographs transmitted by the Belin system. Most of these magazines survived the war. This 1947 *But et club* main story covered Camellini's victory at Briançon with an eight-minute lead over Brambilla.

Special yearly souvenir issues featuring *Tour de France* races are especially precious finds for collectors. Even more so when they are signed by the winner as is this 1948 issue signed by Gino Bartali.

The illustrator Pellos captured the spirit of the sport through his caricatures. The four champions shown here are Hugo Koblet, Louison Bobet, Gino Bartali and Fausto Coppi.

A tri-weekly printed on three different colors of paper, *Miroir sprint* was run by the Communist Party. Cycling events were extensively covered.

NELLO LAUREDI ROI DU DAUPHINÉ

Every spring, *L'Équipe* published a special issue on the upcoming cycling season and the leading athletes.

This view of the pack with the Arc de Triomphe in the background is a reminder that in years past, the *Tour de France* started in Paris and finished there three weeks later.

... AVANT DE GAGNER LES PORTES DE PARIS...

The legendary Fausto Coppi

COPPI reagisce e passa primo in vetta.

le C. CROCE DI FERRO m.2087

Si riforma compatto il gruppo

Zelasco scatta

COPPI primo 2°Ruiz a 2'20" Le Guilly a 2'55" Bartali a 4'30"

Fugge Le Guilly che precede Coppi di 1'30"

St. JEAN DE MAURIENNE m.565

C. TELEGRAFO

Ile C. GALIBIER m.2658

COPPI primo Ruiz a 7'9" Ockers a 9'9" 4° Le Guilly 5° Bartali a circa 13"

ARRIVO SESTRIÈRE

COPPI primo con 4'30" su Robic–5'10" su Ockers e Ruiz 5'55" su Bartali e Le Guilly

Tutti in gruppo i corridori ai pie di del Colle.

C. LAUTARET

MONGINEVRO m.1854

Crolla Robic

Attacco del Galibier. Le Guilly ha 2'20" sugli inseguitori. A metà salita COPPI scatta, pianta tutti, raggiunge Le Guilly, e a 4 km. dalla vetta lo lascia.

CESANA

PARTENZA m.719 BOURG d'OISANS

COPPI primo con 4'40" su Robic–5'25" su Ockers e Ruiz – 6' su Bartali e Close– 6'15" su Le Guilly.

BRIANÇON

Il pittore A. Patitucci illustra la più grande impresa di Fausto Coppi: la strapotente vittoria ottenuta al Sestriere, nel Giro di Francia 1952 che doveva vincere con quasi venti minuti di vantaggio.

L'AQUILOTTO HA SPICCATO IL VOLO

32-33-34

LUGLIO 1954: Coppi si allena sulla Milano-Pavia. Da un autocarro si stacca la ruota di scorta che lo investe.

Prior to the stage between Bourg d'Oisans and Sestrières in the 1952 *Tour de France*, Fausto Coppi was dominating the race. It was the first of the stages to finish in the mountains. Italian readers could easily follow their champion's feats thanks to this remarkable drawing from pre-computer days.

A drawing is worth a thousand words and as many photos. In 1954, Coppi was injured by a spare tire which fell off the back of a truck between Milan and Pavia.

French journalists have always been outdone in the use of hyperbole by their Italian counterparts, especially when Coppi dominated European cycling. His victory in the 1946 Milan-San Remo was heralded by the Italian press in the following manner: "The young eagle has taken wing."

Coppi's name written in enormous letters on the road. Sports journalists call this being a legend of the moment.

IL NOME DI COPPI SU TUTTE LE STRADE
Fausto nel vittorioso Gran Premio Vanini a cronometro del 1952

Coppi's victories in the World Championships in 1949 and 1953 as well as his private audience with Pope Pius XII, far from prying cameras, are presented in spectacular drawings.

FAUSTO COPPI

CAMPIONE INOBLIABILE

SUPPLEMENTO AL N. 10 DEL 10 MARZO 1960 DE «LO SPORT ILLUSTRATO» - SPEDIZ. IN ABBONAMENTO POST. (GRUPPO II)   L. 200

After contracting a mysterious virus while on tour in Africa in 1960, Coppi's untimely death left Italy in shock. The press published special commemorative issues recounting the champion's career.

Pictures big and small

To keep the legend alive and ever present in the mind of children, magazines offered posters of great champions. His three successive wins in the *Tour de France* in the Fifties qualified Louison Bobet as a sport myth.

LOUIS BOBET

RAYMOND MASTROTTO

Raymond Mastrotto never gained star status but was nonetheless an excellent cyclist who assisted the team leaders in their victories. His moment of glory came in his 1967 *Tour de France* win of the Luchon – Pau stage with its difficult ascents. Afterwards he told journalists: "I was sweating so profusely that it lubricated the chain."

World champion track racer Michel Rousseau also had his card in the same series.

Bicycle makers also issued their own series of cards representing the cyclists who used their equipment. Gitane Bicycles was justifiably proud of Daniel Morellon, the greatest French track racer of all times: three Olympic gold medals and eight times world champion.

Club Chocolat Aiglon

13. — KUBLER · KOBLET · GOLDSMITH

Teenagers love chocolate. Teenagers love cycling. Why not put cycling cards inside chocolate bars? Why not also publish collector's album with places for the entire series? In pasting the cards they have, it is so much easier to see which cards are missing. The Swiss champions Ferdie Kubler (left), Hugo Koblet (center), are represented on this card with Goldsmith, from Luxemburg, who never lived up to expectations.

ROGER LEVEQUE sur cycles STELLA

Cycling cards were also popular in other European countries. The German cyclist Rudi Altig is presented on this Schauff Bicycle card. Always present in the final sprint, he owed his success in road and track races to his incredible power of acceleration. Altig was a specialist of the grueling Six Days of Paris in the 1960's.

The makers of Saint-Raphaël, a sweet vermouth, sponsored a well known cycling team. Roger Leveque was one of its faithful members winning several stages in the 1951 *Tour de France*. He also put his stamp of approval on this popular cocktail.

The selling of a champion

Eddy Merckx is the greatest cycling champion of all time. Winning was so instinctive to him that the mere thought of being an also-ran was unbearable. His nickname "The Cannibal" was almost inevitable. Companies competed to have him promote their products. Record companies regularly brought out songs singing his victories. There were also Eddy Merckx cigars and match-books with his photo. Perhaps it seemed normal for him also to promote R6 cigarettes. Considering his enormous youth following, the Eddy Merckx card and figurine game was more logical. Does the good luck sticker mean that his numerous victories were not only due to his sports talent?

For the younger fans

In those days, for several weeks during the summer, young boys and fathers listened to Georges Briquet's live radio coverage of the *Tour de France*. When they went together to cafés, sons tried to decipher the daily results scribbbled on the wall blackboard, while they listened to their fathers analyzing each cyclist's performance for hours. Later they wanted to be professional cyclists and take part in the *Tour de France*. Soon they would receive their first two-wheeler. In the meantime, they used their allowance to buy magazines with comic strips about their favorite champions and somber stories about fierce rivalries behind the scenes.

In fact, the boys were literally submerged in bicycles: on notebook covers, blotters, toys and games. They collected sports figurines and during recess, they competed in *Tour de France* marble games.

This issue of *Francs-Jeux magazine* recounted a famous cycling story that happened during the 1934 *Tour de France*. Although he was the stage leader, René Vietto turned back to help his team leader, Antonin Magne. He gave Magne one of his wheels allowing the team leader to win the *Tour*, while Vietto waited behind for the assistance team. This selfless deed won him incredible popularity with cycling fans. However, bicycle stories for children were most often fictional and like stories of knights or pirates, every race includes sabotage and betrayal.

There were bicycle stories for all ages. For very young children, for example, in one of the adventures of *Dydo*, illustrated by Durane, the hero has a bicycle store. Older children preferred *Olympic* or *The Giants of the Roads* (*Les Géants de la route*) card album. In promotional coloring books like *Louison Bobet, maillot jaune* the life story of champions showed how destiny shaped their careers.

School desks were overrun with bicycle-related advertisements. A leading paint manufacturer, Novémail, reminded children that it was easy to repaint their bikes and La Mère Picon cheese that they organized races. The National Cycling Federation printed their version of bicycling history to guarantee its place in History.

Games and toys

Children do have a life outside of school, yet there as well, the bicycle played a role. Many games used bicycle illustrations, for example, this simple block game from the early 20th century.

Several variations of a very basic and quickly boring game: bicycle roulette for pre-teenagers. Each player chooses a racer and the wheel is spun. Since no money supposedly changed hands, the winner has the simple pleasure of winning.

The *Tour de France* race inspired many family board games played with dice. Perfect for armchair athletes, they also taught players basic geography.

75

The Six Days of Paris was another cycling event which inspired board games. But the players, like the cyclists, soon realized that they were just going around in circles.

With one basic model and different painted panels, this pinball machine (top right and bottom) could be adapted to different countries. This game with ballbearings (top left) demands nerves of steel and could drive a player to smoke, thus the built-in ashtray.
This battery-run cyclist (bottom left) is an ancestor of more recent remote control toys.

Cardboard sheets with cutout figures permitted children to recreate the atmosphere of cycling races, both during the competition and behind the scenes: police vehicles, groups of cheering fans, a falling cyclist, another sleeping in his hotel bed, the last laps around the race track. All that was necessary was a little imagination and a good pair of scissors.

Figurines

Some coffee companies added a plastic figurine in every package. Children could paint them to make them more realistic. Louison Bobet and Fausto Coppi were favorite subjects in the Fifties.

It is difficult for those who have never spent whole afternoons on the beach playing *Tour de France* marble games to understand how important these plastic or lead figurines were for children. First came the work of imagining and building the circuit with hills and mountains. Often the race ended on a circular banked track. Next each player had to choose his cyclist. This was usually the moment when tempers flared over who got to be Louison Bobet. Once these problems solved, the race could start. Each player in turn flicked his cat's eye through the circuit and marked his place with his figurine. Marble control was important because if it left the circuit, the player lost a turn. At the end of the day, figurines were stuffed in pockets and carefully returned to their place on the bedroom shelf.

To make a realistic pack, cyclists in different colors and positions were needed.

Each year new figurines went on sale. A true fan wanted one from each of the different teams.

Even tandem racers had their figurine.

In some track or road races like Bordeaux–Paris, small motorcycles paced each cyclist. These also had their figurine.

Like a circus, the *Tour de France* is a city on wheels. Here are scale models of vehicles sponsored by different companies. Imagination was at a premium.

Television vehicles are omnipresent on the *Tour de France*. Direct coverage started in 1952.

A *Tour de France* spectator can easily get the impression that there are more motorcycles in the race than bicycles. The National Police are present to ensure the safety of the competitors during the race.

The distribution of food satchels and water bottles is handled by the support staff of each team or by employees of the sponsoring company in specially designated.

A complete collection of cycling figurines includes water and satchel boys.

All participants of the *Tour de France* dream of wearing one of the three special jerseys.

To reward his efforts, the winner takes a victory lap when the race finishes on a closed race track.

Blotters

Cycling helps sales even of products which are only remotely related with the sport. Cyclists watch their weight. Easily digested salt-free rusks can interest professional cyclists who eat in difficult conditions. Vitascorbol vitamin C tablets increase energy levels but are they not on the list of harmless performance-enhancing substances like coffee? 1936 world champion Antonin Magne thanks La Frileuse wine for its support.

In the days before computers and e-mail, people put pen and ink to paper when they wrote letters. The blotter was an indispensable accessory to avoid smudges. It was also a wonderful advertising medium since it remained on desks for months, much better than magazines which were flipped through then closed. Many advertisers wanted to associate their products with the positive image of cycling, even when there was no obvious link.

Blotters were also used to promote bicycles in general without any reference to a specific product. Professional cycling organizations sponsored these advertising campaigns. Bicycles are an inexpensive means of transportation which gets you to work quickly, allows you to be independent and keeps you healthy. What more could you ask for?

Hutchinson tires reminded customers that they manufactured tires for all types of two wheel vehicles and that their tires were "more solid than steel". So strong that knives could be sharpened on them.

The famous Rustine rubber patches were often copied by foreign competitors. This blotter appeals to patriots to buy French brands in order to help the economy.

Years ago, the Velocipedic Union of France imposed helmets on cyclists. This is an advertisement for low-priced lightweight Geno-cycle helmets.

It is difficult to praise derailleurs, chains and inner tubes; but it is convincing to know that 12 championship titles and 52 world records were won using Chaluret bicycle parts.

The holy bonds of marriage are compared to the links of a solid Brampton bicycle chain.

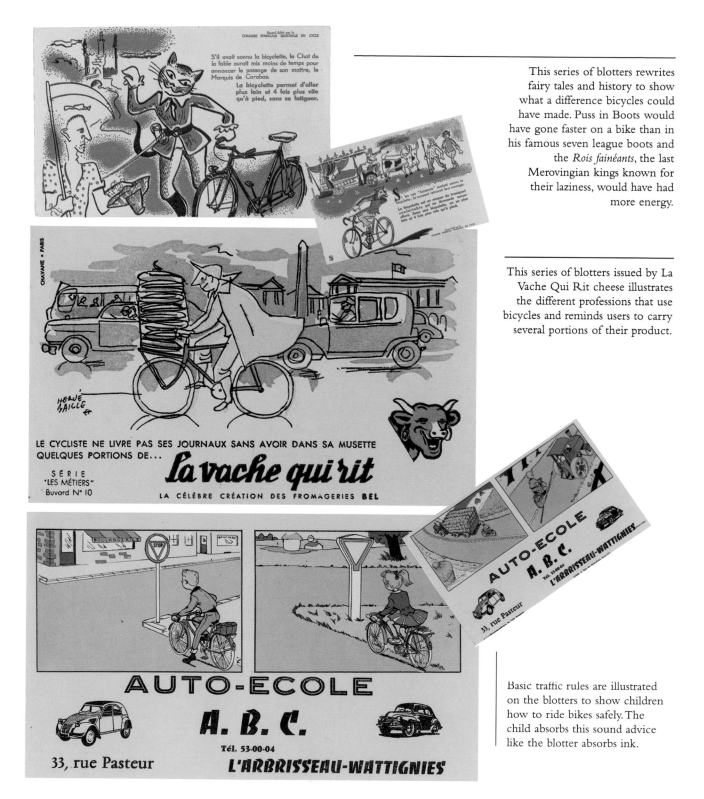

This series of blotters rewrites fairy tales and history to show what a difference bicycles could have made. Puss in Boots would have gone faster on a bike than in his famous seven league boots and the *Rois fainéants*, the last Merovingian kings known for their laziness, would have had more energy.

This series of blotters issued by La Vache Qui Rit cheese illustrates the different professions that use bicycles and reminds users to carry several portions of their product.

Basic traffic rules are illustrated on the blotters to show children how to ride bikes safely. The child absorbs this sound advice like the blotter absorbs ink.

Cycling and decorative plates

Cycling was an obvious subject for series of humorous decorative plates from the early 20th century. A would-be toreador atop a bicycle charges a bull and a hunter on wheels takes advantage of his additional speed to chase down a hare.

An other series of plates show the different stages of the *Tour de France*. These were the types of gifts that spectators could win at the festivities at the end of each race.

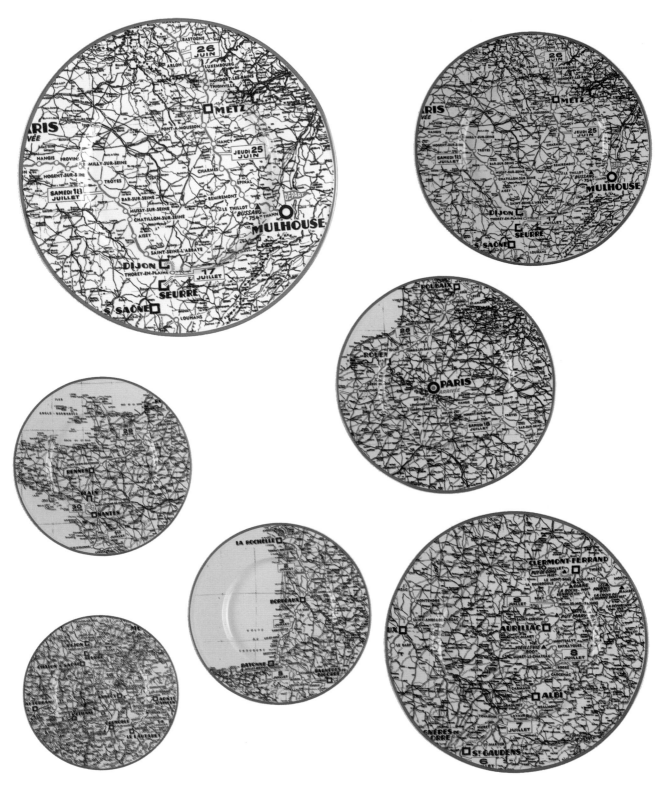

Up in smoke

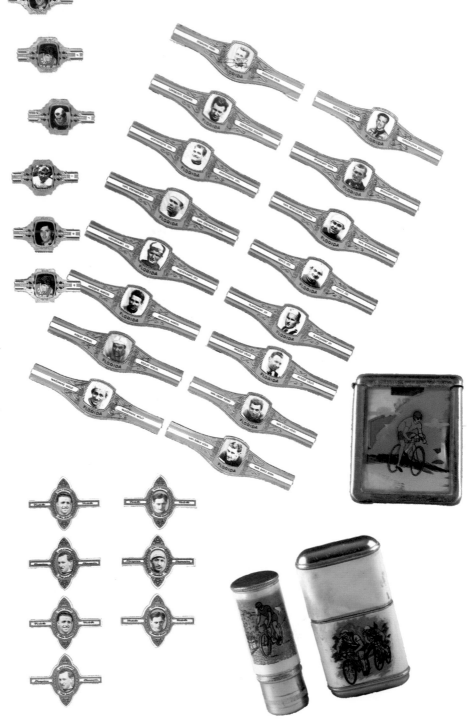

Smoking a cigar among friends, especially those who are also cycling fans, is always pleasurable. When the cigars are special limited editions with bands representing favorite champions, so much the better. The fact that smoking endangers the health seems less important. The bands are valuable collectibles for cycling enthusiasts as well as for those who only collect cigar bands and tobacco-related items.

Belgian smokers could collect matchboxes with pictures of the local cycling champions. They were available at cafés, a common meeting place for fans after races. Not to be outdone, Seita, the state-owned French cigarette manufacturer, issued series of match-books with their cycling champions, including those who won gold medals in the Mexico City Olympic Games.

A last one for the road

Beer mugs are often full to the brim after the finish for thirsty spectators. In 1988, the outdoor world championships took place in Ronse Renaix and were won by the Italian Maurizio Fondriest. Despite their disappointment, Belgian fans were willing to toast his victory.

For non-alcoholic drinkers, Coca Cola, a longtime sponsor of the *Tour de France*, produced limited edition glasses and soda cans. Each of the three special jerseys has its matching glass – yellow, green or red polka dots.

Winning a world championship is a surefire way to have a beer mug with your picture on it. Beheyt won in 1963, his only notable victory, and here is his mug. Tom Simpson, the 1965 champion, had a better record, but is unfortunately remembered by cycling fans for his untimely death during a mountain race in 1967.

This series of wine pitchers is a general tribute to cycling.

These salt-glazed earthenware mugs are decorated with silhouettes of famous cyclists. Rik Van Steenbergen (left) won three world championship titles in 1949, 1956 and 1957. Rik Van Loo (right) was twice world champion in 1960 and 1961.

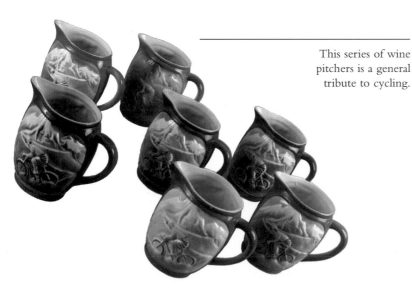

Bibliography

BLANC Jean-Noël. *La légende des cycles,* Éditions Quorum, Paris, 1996.
BLONDIN Antoine. *Sur le tour de France*, Éditions La Table Ronde, Paris, 1996.
BRUNEL Philippe. *Le Tour de France intime: seigneurs et forçats de la route,* Éditions Calmann-Lévy, Paris, 1995.
CHANY Pierre. *La fabuleuse histoire du cyclisme*, Éditions de la Martinière, Paris, 1997.
CHANY Pierre. *La fabuleuse histoire du Tour de France,* Éditions de la Martinière, Paris, 1993.
DODGE Pryor. *La grande histoire du vélo*, Éditions Flammarion, Paris, 1996.
DUFOUR Christian. *L'ABCdaire du vélo*, Éditions Flammarion, Paris, 1997.
JOYCE Dan. *Le grand livre du vélo*, Éditions Solar, Paris, 1998.
LAGET Serge (general editor). *La légende du cyclisme*, Éditions Liber (Switzerland), 1997.
LONDRES Albert. *Tour de France, tour de souffrance*, Le serpent à plumes Editions, Paris, 1996.
PATURLE Hervé. *Un siècle de cyclisme*, Éditions Calmann-Lévy, Paris, 1996.

Useful addresses

Museums
France
Musée du cycle et de la moto, 1 place de la 2ème Division de Cavalerie, 54300 Lunéville.
Germany
Oldenburgen Fahradmuseum, 45 Donnerschweer Strasse, 26123 Oldenburg.
Italy
Cycling Museum, 59 via Papa Giovanni, 24030 Almenno San Bartolomeo (Bergamo).
Great Britain
British Cycling Museum of Camelford, The Old Station Camelford, PL329TZ Cornwall.
United States
Pedaling History Bicycle Museum, Orchard Park, New York.

Web sites
L'Équipe sports magazine: www. lequipe.fr
Le Tour de France: www. letour.fr
L'Union Cycliste Internationale: www. uci.ch
Les cahiers de médiologie: www. mediologie. com. Special issue on cycling.

We would like to thank Charles Guénard for his invaluable help. All the cycling memorabilia presented in this book is from his vast collection.

Games and toys
Postcards
Books and magazines
Records and sheet music
Figurines
Commemorative plates
Jerseys
Racing caps
Water bottles
Objets d'art

Objects from his collection are on sale in his shops in France.

Aux collections du sport
40, avenue Ledru Rollin
75 012 Paris
Telephone: 01 44 73 01 07

5, route de Lyon
89 400 Charmoy
Telephone: 03 86 91 26 43

We would particularly like to thank Marie-Françoise and Jean-Paul Dupont for their generous help. Their association, *Ces merveilleux fous pédalants sur leurs drôles de machines,* kindly allowed us to photograph some of the many antique bicycles in their collection.

Ces merveilleux fous pédalants sur leurs drôles de machines.
6, rue du Puits "Les chevaliers", 17 800 Pons, France. Telephone and fax: 05 46 91 16 19.

We kindly thank the Zéfal Company who allowed us to photograph bicycles from their collection.

Printed in Italy